The

ABC

...of kids cooking

Woman's Day

The

ABC

...of kids cooking

what better way to learn your abc

than by creating a stir in the kitchen!

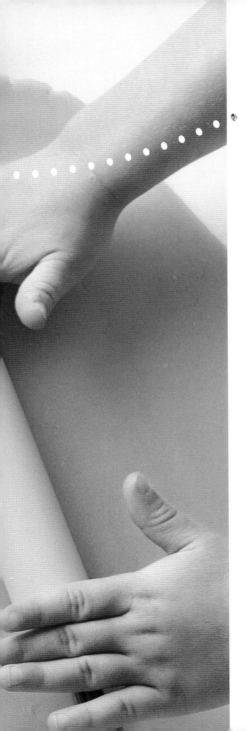

contents

A is for.....

apple turnovers

makes 8
preparation 15 minutes, plus chilling time
cooking 30 minutes

> **40g butter**
> **3 Granny Smith apples, peeled, cored, finely chopped**
> **2 tablespoons maple syrup**
> **1 tablespoon caster sugar**
> **½ teaspoon ground cinnamon**
> **¼ cup sultanas**
> **2 sheets frozen puff pastry, thawed**
> **1 egg, lightly beaten**
> **icing sugar, ice-cream, to serve**

Step 1. Melt butter in a large frying pan over a medium heat. Cook apple, stirring occasionally, for 4-5 minutes until tender. Stir in maple syrup, sugar, and cinnamon. Cook, stirring, for 4-5 minutes until liquid boils and thickens.

Step 2. Transfer mixture to a bowl. Stir in sultanas. Set aside for 15 minutes to cool, then chill until mixture is cold. Preheat oven to hot, 200°C. Cut each pastry sheet into 4 even-sized squares.

Step 3. Spoon 2 tablespoons apple mixture onto one half of each pastry square. Brush edges with a little egg. Fold pastry over filling to form a triangle, pressing edges to seal. Brush with remaining egg. Bake for 15-20 minutes until golden. Dust with icing sugar and serve with ice-cream.

......apple turnover

13

B is for......

banana smoothie

serves 4
preparation 5 minutes

> 2 cups milk, chilled
> 3 ripe bananas, peeled, sliced
> 4 scoops vanilla ice-cream
> ½ cup vanilla
  (or other flavour) yoghurt
> 1 tablespoon honey
> nutmeg, to serve

Step 1. Arrange all the ingredients
on the work surface.
Step 2. Place all ingredients in a blender or
food processor. Process until smooth.
Step 3. Transfer to a jug and pour into glasses.
Serve topped with a sprinkling of nutmeg.

.....banana smoothie

15

C is for..............

cookies

ℂ is for.....

abc cookies

makes 26
preparation 30 minutes, plus chilling time
cooking 20 minutes

> **125g butter, at room temperature, chopped**
> **½ cup caster sugar**
> **1 egg yolk**
> **2 cups plain flour**
> **1 teaspoon bicarbonate of soda**
> **¼ cup honey**

Step 1. Preheat oven to moderate, 180°C. Lightly grease and line 4 baking trays with baking paper. In a large bowl, using an electric mixer, beat together butter and sugar for 2-3 minutes until creamy. Add egg yolk, beating well. Fold in combined sifted flour and bicarbonate of soda.

Step 2. Heat honey in a microwave-safe bowl in the microwave on high (100%) power for 20 seconds. Stir into dough. Mix well. Cover in plastic wrap. Chill for 30 minutes. Knead gently on a lightly floured surface. Roll out between 2 sheets of baking paper until 0.5cm thick.

Step 3. Using 8cm alphabet cutters, cut out letters. Place on prepared trays. Bake for 15-20 minutes until firm to touch. Allow to cool on trays. Spread with icing (see note) and decorate.

note

To make icing, beat 1 egg white with a wooden spoon until frothy. Add 1¼ cups sifted pure icing sugar, 1 tablespoonful at a time, beating well after each addition. When icing is a piping consistency, mix in a few drops of lemon juice. Add colouring of your choice.

.....cookies

D is for....

damper rolls

makes 6
preparation 10 minutes
cooking 15 minutes

> 2 cups self-raising flour
> 30g butter
> 1 cup grated tasty cheese
> ¾ cup rolled oats
> ½ cup milk
> ½ cup water
> 1 tablespoon snipped chives

Step 1. Preheat oven to very hot, 220°C.
Lightly grease a baking tray. Sift flour into
a bowl. Add butter. Using fingertips, lightly
rub in until mixture is combined. Mix in ½ cup
cheese and ½ cup oats. Make a well in centre.
Step 2. In a jug, combine the milk and water.
Pour into the well all at once, reserving
1 tablespoon of liquid. Using a palette knife,
quickly mix to a soft, sticky dough. Do not
over-mix. Turn onto a lightly floured work
surface. Knead lightly. Divide dough into
6 even-sized pieces.
Step 3. Lightly knead each piece into a ball,
pressing out slightly. Place close together on
prepared tray. Brush rolls with reserved milk
mixture. In a bowl, combine remaining cheese,
remaining oats and chives. Sprinkle over rolls.
Bake for 12-15 minutes until rolls sound
hollow when tapped. Allow to cool on a wire
rack. Serve.

......damper

E is for............

egg bake

E is for......

egg bake

makes 4
preparation 10 minutes
cooking 30 minutes

> **2 teaspoons vegetable oil**
> **2 rashers rindless bacon,
>   finely chopped**
> **½ small red onion, finely chopped**
> **125g cherry tomatoes, halved**
> **8 eggs**
> **⅔ cup grated tasty cheese**
> **2 tablespoons finely chopped chives**
> **2 tablespoons finely chopped parsley**

Step 1. Preheat oven to moderately slow,
160°C. Lightly grease 4 x 1½-cup ramekins.
Arrange on a baking tray. Heat oil in
a medium frying pan on high. Sauté bacon
and onion for 3-4 minutes until onion is
tender. Add tomato and cook 1 minute.
Allow to cool.
Step 2. In a bowl, combine bacon mixture,
4 eggs, half the cheese, chives and parsley.
Season to taste. Divide evenly between
prepared ramekins.
Step 3. Break remaining eggs, one at a time,
into a small bowl. Carefully slide one into
each dish. Sprinkle each evenly with remaining
cheese. Bake for 20-25 minutes until the yolk
is just set. Serve.

egg bake

F is for.....

fish fingers
with wedges

serves 4
preparation 20 minutes
cooking 35 minutes

> 4 potatoes, peeled, cut into wedges
> 1 tablespoon olive oil
> 600g white skinless boneless fish fillets (such as ling or perch), cut crossways into 3cm-wide pieces
> ¼ cup seasoned flour
> ⅓ cup milk
> 1 egg, lightly beaten
> 1 cup dry breadcrumbs
> mayonnaise, lemon wedges, to serve

Step 1. Preheat oven to very hot, 220°C. Line 2 baking trays with baking paper. In a large bowl, toss potato in oil. Season to taste. Place in a single layer on one of the prepared trays. Bake for 20 minutes.
Step 2. Meanwhile, toss fish in flour and shake off excess. Dip into combined milk and egg. Dip into breadcrumbs, pressing firmly. Place on other tray. Spray with oil.
Step 3. Bake fish and potato wedges for a further 10-15 minutes until golden and cooked through, turning fish fingers halfway through cooking. Serve with mayonnaise and lemon wedges.

.....fish fingers

27

G is for......

guacamole

makes about 2 cups
preparation 10 minutes
cooking 10 minutes

> 6 flour tortillas
> vegetable sticks of choice
  (carrot, celery, green beans)
  GUACAMOLE
> 2 ripe avocados, halved,
  stones removed, peeled
> 1 onion, finely chopped
> 1 large tomato, chopped
> ¼ cup light sour cream
> juice 1 lime or ½ lemon
> 1 garlic clove, crushed

Step 1. Preheat oven to moderate, 180°C.
Line a baking tray with baking paper. Arrange
tortillas on prepared tray. Spray with oil.
Step 3. Bake for 5-10 minutes or until crisp,
then allow to cool. Break tortillas into pieces.
Step 3. GUACAMOLE: In a bowl, lightly mash
avocado with a fork and blend in all remaining
ingredients. Season to taste. Serve as a dip
for crispy tortillas and vegetable sticks.

tip
For easy mashing it is important that the
avocados are very ripe.

guacamole

H is for.....

hamburger
with the lot

makes 4
preparation 20 minutes, plus chilling time
cooking 10 minutes

- › 500g beef mince
- › 1 small brown onion, finely chopped
- › 2 tablespoons finely chopped parsley
- › 1 egg, lightly beaten
- › 2 garlic cloves, crushed
- › 1 tablespoon oil
- › 4 slices tasty cheese
- › 4 bacon rashers
- › 4 rolls, halved, toasted
- › 1/3 cup tomato sauce
- › 4 butter lettuce leaves
- › 2 tomatoes, thinly sliced
- › chips, to serve

Step 1. In a medium bowl, combine beef, onion, parsley, egg and garlic. Season to taste. Shape mixture into 4 evenly-sized flattened patties. Place on a tray. Cover and chill for 15 minutes until firm.

Step 2. Heat oil in a large frying pan on medium. Fry patties for 3-5 minutes each side until cooked through.

Step 3. Top each patty with a slice of cheese. Set aside and cover to keep warm. Fry bacon in the same pan over a high heat for 2-3 minutes each side until crisp. Spread tomato sauce on roll bases. Top each with lettuce, tomato, a patty, bacon and remaining half of roll. Serve hamburgers with chips.

hamburger

is for...............

ice-cream

I is for......

ice-cream
sandwiches

makes 6
preparation 10 minutes

> **12 chocolate chip biscuits**
> **6 small scoops chocolate ice-cream**
> **granulated peanuts (see note), hundreds and thousands, to coat**

Step 1. Line a baking tray with baking paper. Sandwich 2 biscuits together with 1 scoop ice-cream.
Step 2. Using a knife, carefully cut away any excess ice-cream.
Step 3. Place peanuts and hundreds and thousands in separate bowls. Roll ice-cream sandwiches, upright, in peanuts , then in hundreds and thousands, ensuring ice-cream is evenly coated. Arrange ice-cream sandwiches on tray and freeze until required.

note
Remember to check that no-one has an allergy to nuts. If you're not sure, use chocolate sprinkles instead of nuts.

....ice-cream

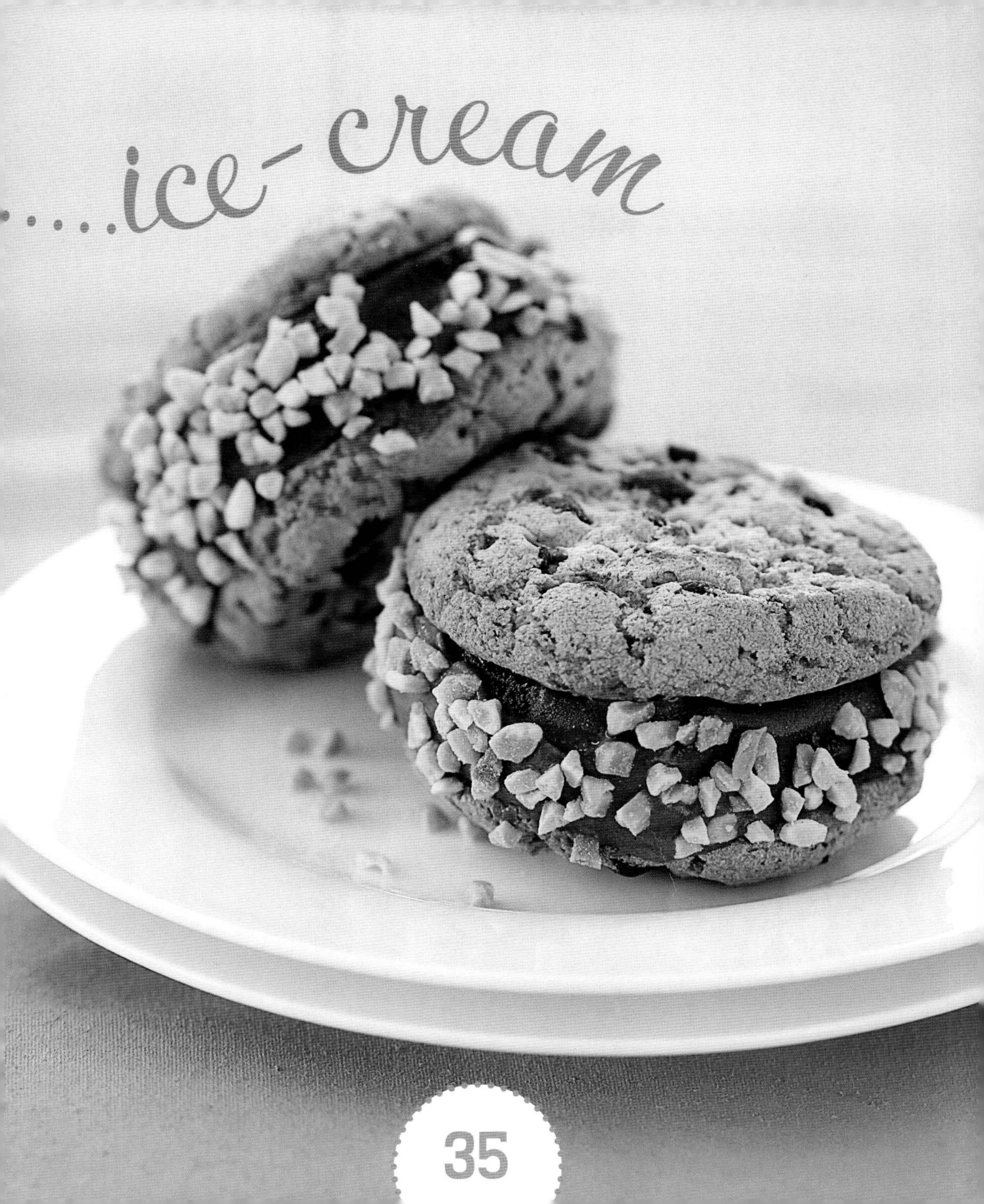

vanilla ice-cream

serves 6
preparation 10 minutes, plus
overnight freezing

> 395g can sweetened condensed milk
> 300g carton sour cream
> 3 teaspoons vanilla extract
> 2 egg whites
> ice-cream cones, to serve

Step 1. Line a metal cake pan
with plastic wrap. In a large bowl,
whisk together condensed milk,
sour cream and vanilla extract.
Step 2. In another bowl, using
an electric mixer, beat egg whites
until soft peaks form. Fold into milk
mixture. Pour into prepared pan.
Step 3. Cover with plastic wrap and
freeze overnight until firm. Serve
scoops of ice-cream in cones.

strawberry sundaes

serves 6
preparation 5 minutes

> 12 scoops strawberry ice-cream
> 12 strawberries, hulled, chopped
> Ice Magic

Step 1. Place 2 scoops ice-cream
into each dish.
Step 2. Top with strawberries.
Step 3. Drizzle with
Ice Magic to serve.

tip
These sundaes
are extra yummy
when served with
ice-cream wafers.

hokey-pokey ice-cream

serves 6
preparation 5 minutes, plus
overnight freezing

> ½ litre vanilla ice-cream,
  slightly softened
> ⅓ cup caramel topping
> 2 Violet Crumbles, chopped

Step 1. In a bowl, combine ice-cream,
caramel topping and three-quarters
of the Violet Crumble. Mix well.
Step 2. Spoon into a metal cake pan.
Cover and freeze overnight until firm.
Step 3. Serve scoops of ice-cream
topped with remaining Violet Crumble.

rainbow ice-cream

serves 6
preparation 5 minutes, plus
overnight freezing

> ½ litre vanilla ice-cream,
  softened slightly
> ½ cup coloured sprinkles
> ice-cream cones, to serve

Step 1. In a large bowl, combine
the ice-cream and sprinkles.
Step 2. Spoon into a metal cake pan.
Step 3. Cover and freeze overnight
until firm. Serve scoops of rainbow
ice-cream in cones.

I is for.........

ice-cream

37

is for.......

jelly oranges

makes 8
preparation 20 minutes, plus chilling time
cooking 12 minutes

> **4 oranges**
> **½ cup caster sugar**
> **3 teaspoons gelatine**
> **½ cup just-boiled water**

Step 1. Cut oranges in half. Juice and strain into a jug. Scrape flesh from skins. Place skins in a bowl and cover with boiling water. Stand for 1 minute before draining and rinsing under cold water. Place on a wire rack and drain well.
Step 2. In a small saucepan, combine orange juice and sugar. Stir over a low heat until sugar dissolves. Bring to the boil over a high heat. Reduce heat to low and simmer for 10 minutes.
Step 3. Place orange halves in 8 recesses of a 12-hole muffin pan. In a small jug, using a fork, whisk gelatine briskly into just-boiled water until dissolved. Remove from heat. Blend gelatine mixture into orange mixture in pan. Pour into orange skins. Chill for 3 hours or overnight until set. Serve whole or cut into wedges.

tip
Make these a day in advance to ensure they are well chilled and firm.

jelly oranges

K is for............

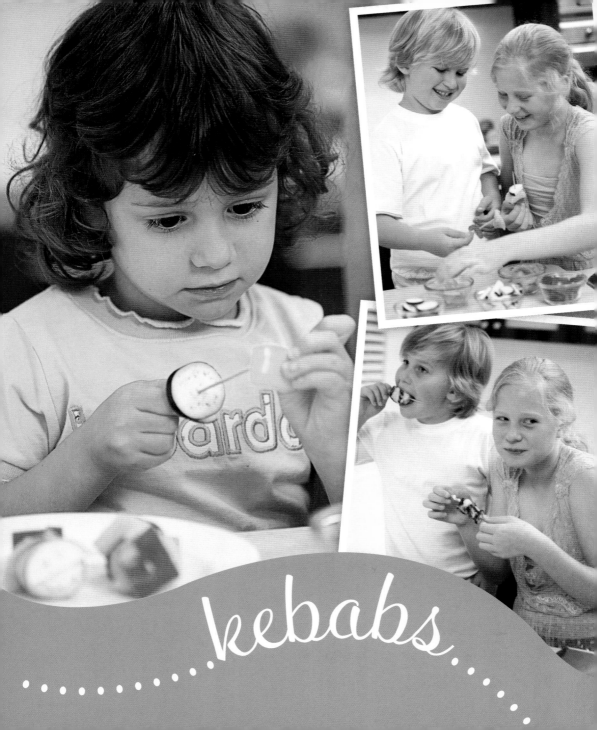

kebabs

K is for......

chicken kebabs
with potato & pesto

makes 12
preparation 20 minutes
cooking 25 minutes

> 1kg baby new potatoes, unpeeled
> 50g butter, chopped
> 1 tablespoon milk
> 500g chicken breast, cut into 2cm cubes
> 1 zucchini, halved lengthways, sliced
> 1 baby eggplant, sliced
> ½ red capsicum, seeded, cut into 2cm cubes
> ½ yellow capsicum, seeded, cut into 2cm cubes
> 6 bamboo skewers, halved, soaked
> 1 tablespoons olive oil
> ready-made pesto, to serve

Step 1. Cook potatoes in a saucepan of boiling, salted water for 15-20 minutes until tender. Drain. Transfer half the potatoes to a medium bowl. Mash with butter and milk until smooth. Roughly mash remaining potatoes. Fold into mash mixture. Season to taste. Keep warm.
Step 2. Meanwhile, thread chicken and vegetables alternately onto skewers. Brush with oil and season to taste.
Step 3. Spray a char-grill with oil. Preheat on medium. Cook skewers for 3-5 minutes each side until chicken is cooked through. Serve with mash and pesto.

kebabs

43

lamb kebabs

makes 8
preparation 20 minutes,
plus marinating time
cooking 12 minutes

> **500g lamb backstrap, cubed**
> **⅓ cup vegetable stock**
> **1 tablespoon Dijon mustard**
> **1 garlic clove, crushed**
> **1 punnet grape tomatoes**
> **1 red onion, cut into wedges**
> **8 bamboo skewers, soaked**
> **couscous, to serve**

Step 1. In a bowl, combine lamb, wine, mustard and garlic. Season to taste. Marinate for 30 minutes.
Step 2. Thread lamb, tomatoes and onion onto skewers. Char-grill skewers for 10-12 minutes, turning, until cooked to taste. Serve with coucous.

lime fish kebabs

makes 8
preparation 15 minutes
cooking 10 minutes

> **finely grated rind and juice 1 lime**
> **1 garlic clove, crushed**
> **600g blue-eye travalla, cubed**
> **1 red capsicum, seeded, cubed**
> **8 bamboo skewers, soaked**
> **cooked rice, lime wedges, to serve**

Step 1. In a bowl, combine lime rind, lime juice and garlic. Add fish. Cover. Chill for 10 minutes.
Step 2. Thread fish and capsicum onto skewers. Season to taste. Chargrill skewers for 8-10 minutes, turning, until cooked through. Serve with rice and lime wedges.

soy chicken kebabs

makes 16
preparation 10 minutes,
plus chilling time
cooking 15 minutes

> **500g chicken breast fillets, cut into 16 strips**
> **16 bamboo skewers, soaked**
> **¼ cup mirin**
> **2 tablespoons brown sugar**
> **2 tablespoons soy sauce**
> **1 green onion, sliced thinly**

Step 1. Thread chicken onto skewers. Place in a baking dish with mirin, sugar and sauce soy. Chill overnight.
Step 2. Chargrill skewers, reserving marinade, for 8-10 minutes, turning, until cooked through.
Step 3. Simmer reserved marinade for 3-5 minutes until thickened. Drizzle over skewers. Top with onion.

cheese & ham kebabs

makes 8
preparation 20 minutes
cooking 10 minutes

> **1 loaf ciabatta bread, cubed**
> **¼ cup olive oil**
> **8 bamboo skewers, soaked**
> **16 slices shaved ham, folded**
> **250g haloumi cheese, cubed**
> **8 cherry tomatoes**

Step 1. Toss bread in oil. Thread bread and remaining ingredients onto skewers. Char-grill skewers for 8-10 minutes, turning, until golden.

K is for......

....kebabs

45

L is for......

lamingtons

makes 24
preparation 30 minutes
cooking 5 minutes

> **450g plain Madeira
>   or sponge cake, trimmed**
> **4 cups icing sugar mixture**
> **½ cup cocoa powder**
> **⅔ cup milk**
> **20g butter, melted**
> **2 cups shredded coconut**

Step 1. Cut cake into 24 x 3cm pieces.
Sift icing sugar mixture and cocoa powder
together into a large, heatproof bowl. Stir
in milk and butter. Mix until smooth.
Step 2. Place the bowl over a saucepan of
simmering water and heat on low, stirring,
until sugar dissolves and the mixture is of
a coating consistency.
Step 3. Place coconut in a bowl. Using a fork,
dip cake pieces into chocolate icing. Drain
off excess. Roll in coconut to coat. Place on
a wire rack and allow to set.

note
If the icing becomes too thick, place over
a bowl of warm water.

lamingtons

47

M is for.....

choc-caramel
surprise muffins

makes 12
preparation 15 minutes
cooking 25 minutes

- › **2 cups self-raising flour**
- › **½ cup caster sugar**
- › **½ cup finely chopped pecans**
- › **100g dark chocolate, grated**
- › **⅔ cup milk**
- › **125g butter, melted**
- › **1 egg, lightly beaten**
- › **6 jersey caramels, halved**

Step 1. Preheat oven to moderate, 180°C. Lightly grease a 12-hole muffin pan. Sift flour into a large bowl. Stir in sugar, pecans and chocolate.

Step 2. In a jug, whisk together milk, butter and egg. Make a well in the centre of flour mixture. Add milk mixture all at once. Mix lightly until just combined – don't over-mix.

Step 3. Spoon enough mixture into each recess of prepared pan to half fill. Top each with half a caramel. Cover evenly with remaining muffin mixture. Bake for 20-25 minutes or until a skewer inserted into the centre comes out clean and dry. Transfer to a wire rack to cool.

tip
To experience the surprise inside, these muffins are best served warm. Other sweets of choice, such as Rollos or squares of Caramello chocolate, can be used.

.....muffins

cheesy kumara muffins

makes 12
preparation 15 minutes
cooking 30 minutes

> 2 cups self-raising flour, sifted
> 1 cup grated kumara, firmly packed
> 2 tablespoons snipped chives
> ⅔ cup buttermilk
> 125g butter, melted
> 1 egg, lightly beaten
> 125g tasty cheese, cut into 12 cubes

Step 1. Preheat oven to 180°C. Combine flour, kumara and half the chives.
Step 2. Add buttermilk, butter and egg. Mix lightly. Spoon into a greased muffin pan. Press a cube of cheese into each.
Step 3. Sprinkle with chives. Bake for 25-30 minutes.

honey & oat muffins

makes 12
preparation 10 minutes
cooking 25 minutes

> 2½ cups self-raising flour, sifted
> 1 cup caster sugar
> 1 cup rolled oats
> 90g butter
> ¼ cup honey
> 1¼ cups buttermilk
> 1 egg, lightly beaten

Step 1. Preheat oven to 180°C. Combine flour, sugar and ¾ cup oats.
Step 2. Melt butter and honey together. Add to flour mixture with buttermilk and egg.
Step 3. Spoon into a greased muffin pan. Sprinkle with oats. Bake for 20-25 minutes.

marshmallow muffins

makes 12
preparation 15 minutes
cooking 25 minutes

> 2 cups self-raising flour, sifted
> ½ cup caster sugar
> 1 cup frozen mixed berries
> ⅔ cup milk
> 125g butter, melted
> 1 egg, lightly beaten
> 6 pink marshmallows, halved

Step 1. Preheat oven to 180°C. Combine flour, sugar and berries.
Step 2. Add milk, butter and egg. Spoon half into a greased muffin pan. Top with marshmallow halves. Top with batter. Bake for 20-25 minutes.

pineapple muffins

makes 12
preparation 15 minutes
cooking 25 minutes

> 2 cups self-raising flour, sifted
> 1 cup grated tasty cheese
> 100g sliced ham, chopped
> 4 pineapple rings, chopped
> ¼ cup chopped parsley
> ⅔ cup milk
> 125g butter, melted, cooled
> 1 egg, lightly beaten

Step 1. Preheat oven to 180°C. Combine flour, cheese, ham, pineapple and parsley. Add milk, butter and egg.
Step 2. Spoon into a greased muffin pan. Bake for 20-25 minutes.

m is for.....

is for............

nachos

N is for.....

nachos

serves 4 to 6
cooking 10 minutes

> 1 large avocado, halved, stone removed
> 2 teaspoons lemon juice
> 420g can Mexican beans
> ¾ cup refried beans (see tip)
> 230g packet original corn chips
> 1 cup grated tasty cheese
> ½ cup light sour cream

Step 1. Preheat oven to hot, 200°C. Lightly grease 4-6 individual ovenproof dishes. In a small bowl, mash avocado with lemon juice. Season to taste. In a bowl, combine Mexican and refried beans. Divide corn chips among dishes.
Step 2. Spoon bean mixture over corn chips. Top evenly with avocado.
Step 3. Sprinkle with cheese. Arrange dishes on a baking tray. Bake for 5-10 minutes until cheese melts and beans are heated through. Top with a dollop of sour cream to serve.

....nachos

O is for.....

omelette with herbs

serves 4
preparation 15 minutes
cooking 20 minutes

> **8 eggs**
> **½ cup chopped mixed herbs (parsley, chives, chervil)**
> **½ cup grated cheddar cheese**
> **3 green onions, sliced**
> **15g butter, chopped**
> **chervil sprigs, to serve**

Step 1. In a large bowl, whisk egg, herbs, cheese and onion. Transfer mixture to a jug.
Step 2. Heat a knob of butter in a 20cm frying pan on high, swirling to cover base. Pour a quarter of omelette mixture into pan and cook for 2-3 minutes until it begins to set.
Step 3. Fold omelette over and slide onto plate. Serve topped with chervil sprigs. Repeat with remaining mixture and butter.

tip
Other flavourings may be added – try ham, tomato and mushroom. Serve with a salad for an easy, light meal.

omelette

P is for..........

pizza

P is for.....

pizza faces

makes 4
preparation 10 minutes
cooking 10 minutes

> 2 small prepared pizza bases
> ½ cup tomato pasta sauce
> 1 cup grated pizza cheese
> 8 stuffed olives (for eyes)
> 4 slices cabanossi (for noses)
> 4 slices red capsicum (for mouths)
> 8 slices button mushrooms (for ears)
> ⅓ cup chopped rindless bacon (for hair)

Step 1. Preheat oven to hot, 200°C. Line a baking tray with baking paper. Cut 2 x 12cm rounds from each pizza base.
Step 2. Spread each with pasta sauce. Place on prepared tray. Sprinkle with cheese.
Step 3. Arrange ingredients on bases to make faces. Bake for 5-10 minutes until golden and the bases are crisp.

...pizza

61

P is for.....

tomato, pumpkin
& rocket pizza

makes 2
preparation 15 minutes
cooking 45 minutes

> 500g pumpkin, peeled, cubed
> 1 tablespoon olive oil
> 2 sheets frozen shortcrust pastry, thawed
> ½ cup tomato pasta sauce
> 1 cup grated mozzarella
> 200g punnet cherry tomatoes
> 1 red capsicum, seeded, finely chopped
> 40g baby rocket leaves

Step 1. Preheat oven to hot, 200°C. Toss pumpkin with oil in a baking tray. Bake for 25-30 minutes until tender. Set aside.
Step 2. Meanwhile, halfway through cooking pumpkin, lightly grease 2 pizza trays. Cut a 20cm round from each pastry sheet. Place on prepared trays. Prick pastry with a fork and bake for 10 minutes.
Step 3. Spread each pastry round with tomato pasta sauce. Sprinkle with half the cheese. Top with tomatoes, capsicum and pumpkin. Sprinkle with remaining cheese. Bake for 10-15 minutes until golden and the bases are crisp. Top with rocket. Cut into wedges to serve.

....pizza

63

P is for.....

supreme pizza

makes 2
preparation 15 minutes
cooking 10 minutes

> 2 cups self-raising flour
> 30g butter, chopped
> ½ cup milk
> ½ cup water
  TOPPING
> ⅓ cup tomato pasta sauce
> 1½ cups grated pizza cheese
> 1 cup sliced cabanossi
> 1 red capsicum, seeded, thinly sliced
> 1 cup thinly sliced button mushrooms
> 100g shaved ham, chopped

Step 1. Preheat oven to very hot, 220°C. Lightly grease 2 pizza trays. Sift flour into a bowl. Add butter. Using fingertips, rub in lightly. Make a well in centre of flour mixture. Pour in combined milk and water. Using a palette knife, mix quickly to a soft, sticky dough. Don't over-mix.
Step 2. Turn onto a lightly floured surface. Knead lightly. Divide dough into 2 even-sized pieces. Press or roll out each piece until large enough to cover pizza trays (see note).
Step 3. TOPPING: Spread pizza bases evenly with tomato pasta sauce. Cover each with cheese and top with an even amount of cabanossi, capsicum, mushroom and ham. Bake for 10-12 minutes until golden and the bases are crisp. Cut into wedges to serve.

note
This is a scone pizza dough. We've also used it in the Mexican twists recipe on page 66.

pizza

65

P is for.........

mexican twists

serves 16
preparation 15 minutes
cooking 15 minutes

> **1 quantity scone pizza dough
(see Supreme pizza recipe, page 64)**
> **½ cup refried beans**
> **½ cup tomato salsa**
> **1 cup grated tasty cheese**
> **1 tablespoon chopped parsley**
> **milk, to glaze**
> **sesame seeds, to garnish**

Step 1. Preheat oven to hot, 200°C. Line 2 baking
trays with baking paper. Divide dough into 16
even-sized pieces. On a lightly floured surface,
press or roll out into rounds about 0.5cm thick.
Step 2. In a small bowl, combine beans and
tomato salsa. Spread evenly over rounds.
Top with cheese and parsley.
Step 3. Roll up and twist. Place on prepared trays.
Brush with milk. Sprinkle with sesame seeds.
Bake for 10-15 minutes until the twists are golden.

tip
The twists can be made using pastry as the base
– it might be easier for smaller hands to handle.

pizza

Q is for....

quesadilla
– three ways

serves 4 as a snack
preparation 5 minutes
cooking 5 minutes

> **2 flour tortillas**
  BAKED BEANS & CHEESE FILLING
> **½ cup baked beans**
> **⅓ cup grated tasty cheese**
  TOMATO, CHEESE & CHUTNEY FILLING
> **1 tomato, sliced**
> **¼ cup grated tasty cheese**
> **2 tablespoons chutney**
  CHICKEN, CHEESE & SALSA FILLING
> **¼ cup shredded barbecued chicken**
> **¼ cup grated tasty cheese**
> **2 tablespoons tomato salsa**

Step 1. Heat a frying pan on medium with cooking oil. Place 1 tortilla in pan and top with filling of your choice.
Step 2. Cover with the second tortilla and cook for 3-4 minutes, turning once, until golden and crispy.
Step 2. Using a lifter, transfer to a chopping board. Serve warm, cut into quarters.

tips
You can make these with sliced sandwich loaf or Turkish bread instead of the tortillas. Use a sandwich press, if you like.

.....quesadilla

is for.............

rissoles

R is for....

rissoles & mash

makes 8
preparation 15 minutes, plus chilling time
cooking 10 minutes

> 500g lean beef mince
> ½ cup fresh breadcrumbs
> 1 red onion, grated
> 1 egg
> 2 tablespoons chopped parsley, plus extra to serve
> 1 tablespoon barbecue sauce
> 1 garlic clove, crushed
> 1 tablespoon olive oil
> mashed potato (see tip), green beans, gravy, to serve

Step 1. In a bowl, combine mince, breadcrumbs, onion, egg, parsley, barbecue sauce and garlic. Season to taste. Shape mixture into 8 even-sized flattened rissoles.

Step 2. Place rissoles on a baking tray and chill for 15 minutes. Heat oil in a large frying pan on medium.

Step 3. Cook rissoles for 4-5 minutes each side until golden and cooked through. Drain on paper towel. Serve with mashed potato, green beans (or other vegetables) and gravy of your choice. Sprinkle with extra chopped parsley to serve.

tips

For perfect mash, boil peeled, cubed potatoes for 15-20 minutes until very tender. Drain well. Mash with butter and milk or cream. Season to taste. You could also add grated cheese. Make smaller bite-sized rissoles, if you like.

rissoles

S is for......

sausage rolls

makes 18
preparation 20 minutes
cooking 25 minutes

> 250g sausage mince
> 250g beef mince
> 1 small onion, finely chopped
> 1 small carrot, coarsely grated
> 1 small zucchini, coarsely grated
> ½ cup fresh breadcrumbs
> 1 tablespoon tomato paste
> 1 tablespoon barbecue sauce
> 2 eggs, beaten
> 3 sheets frozen puff pastry, thawed
> tomato sauce, to serve

Step 1. Preheat oven to hot, 200°C. Lightly grease and line 2 baking trays. In a large bowl, combine sausage mince, beef mince, onion, carrot, zucchini, breadcrumbs, tomato paste, barbecue sauce and half the egg. Season to taste.
Step 2. Cut each sheet of pastry in half. Roll mixture into 6 long sausage shapes. Place each sausage along the edge of each pastry sheet and roll up tightly to seal.
Step 3. Cut each sausage into 3 even-sized pieces. Place on prepared trays about 3cm apart. Brush with remaining egg. Score tops of pastry in a few places. Bake for 20-25 minutes until golden and cooked through. Serve with tomato sauce.

tip
You can freeze uncooked sausage rolls in an airtight container for up to 2 months.

.....sausage rolls

T is for........

tuna salad

serves 4
preparation 15 minutes
cooking 5 minutes

> **2 corncobs, husk removed**
> **2 cups cooked rice**
> **425g can tuna in springwater, drained**
> **150g tasty cheese, cubed**
> **½ punnet cherry tomatoes, halved**
> **1 Lebanese cucumber, chopped**
> **1 stalk celery, thinly sliced**
> **3 green onions, trimmed, thinly sliced**
> **2 tablespoons dressing of your choice**

Step 1. Slice kernels from corncobs. Add to a saucepan of boiling water. Cook for 4-5 minutes until tender. Drain.
Step 2. In a large bowl, combine corn, rice, tuna, cheese, tomato, cucumber, celery and onion. Season to taste.
Step 3. To serve, pour dressing over salad and toss to combine.

tips
To make this easier to prepare, you can use a 310g can of corn kernels. It's a great lunch box filler and will keep in the fridge for up to 2-3 days in an airtight container.

......tuna salad

U is for.....

upside-down
caramel pear cake

preparation 15 minutes
cooking 35 minutes

- › **125g butter, chopped, at room temperature**
- › **1¼ cups brown sugar**
- › **2 corella pears, peeled, thinly sliced lengthways**
- › **2 eggs**
- › **1 cup self-raising flour, sifted**
- › **1 teaspoon ground cinnamon**
- › **⅓ cup cream**
- › **vanilla ice-cream or thick cream, to serve**

Step 1. Preheat oven to moderate, 180°C. Lightly grease a 22cm fluted ring cake pan. In a small saucepan, combine 60g butter and ¾ cup sugar. Stir over low heat for 2-3 minutes until butter melts and mixture is smooth. Pour into cake pan, tilting to cover base.

Step 2. Arrange pears in caramel, slightly overlapping. Set aside. In a bowl, using an electric mixer, beat remaining butter and sugar until pale and creamy. Add eggs, one at a time, beating well after each addition. Fold in combined flour and cinnamon. Stir in cream.

Step 3. Spoon mixture over pear and smooth top. Bake for 25-30 minutes or until a skewer inserted into the centre comes out clean and dry. Allow to cool in pan for 5 minutes. Turn onto a serving plate. Serve warm or at room temperature, cut into wedges, with ice-cream or cream.

.....upside-down cake

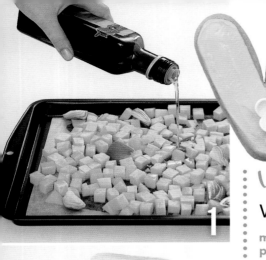

V is for......

vegie dip
with crouton animals

makes 1 cup
preparation 15 minutes
cooking 20 minutes

> **500g butternut pumpkin, peeled,
>   cut into small cubes, roasted**
> **2 eschalots, peeled, quartered**
> **2 tablespoons olive oil, plus extra to brush**
> **6 slices white bread**
> **50g cream cheese, at room temperature**

Step 1. Preheat oven to a hot, 200°C.
Place pumpkin and eschalot on a baking
tray. Drizzle with oil. Season to taste and
toss well. Bake for 15-20 minutes until
pumpkin is tender. Allow to cool.
Step 2. Meanwhile, using animal shape
cookie cutters, cut the bread into shapes.
Arrange in a single layer on a baking tray
and brush with olive oil. Bake for 4-5 minutes
each side until crisp.
Step 3. Spoon pumpkin mixture and cream
cheese into a food processor or blender.
Process until smooth. Season to taste.
Serve dip with crouton shapes. .

tips
If the dip is too thick, add a little water
while blending. Use spray oil when making
croutons if you like.

vegie dip

W is for....

waffles with
caramel banana

serves 4
preparation 5 minutes
cooking 20 minutes

> **1 cup caster sugar**
> **½ cup water**
> **½ cup thickened cream**
> **8 frozen waffles, toasted**
> **2 large bananas, diagonally sliced**
> **thick cream, to serve (optional)**

Step 1. In a saucepan, combine sugar and water. Stir over a medium heat until sugar dissolves. Bring to the boil.
Step 2. Reduce heat to low and simmer, without stirring, for 10-15 minutes until mixture is golden.
Step 3. Remove from heat. Whisk in cream. Return pan to low heat and stir until smooth. Top waffles with banana. Pour over caramel to serve. Accompany with cream, if you like.

waffles

X is for.........

gingerbread shapes

makes about 20
preparation 30 minutes
cooking 15 minutes

> **125g butter, chopped, at room temperature**
> **½ cup caster sugar**
> **1 egg yolk**
> **2 cups plain flour**
> **3 teaspoons ground ginger**
> **1 teaspoon bicarbonate of soda**
> **¼ cup golden syrup**

Step 1. Preheat oven to moderate, 180°C. Lightly grease and line 2 baking trays with baking paper. In a large bowl, using an electric mixer, beat butter and sugar together for 2-3 minutes until creamy. Add egg yolk, beating well.

Step 2. Sift flour, ginger and bicarbonate of soda together. Warm syrup in the microwave on high (100%) power for 20 seconds. Fold flour mixture into butter mixture with syrup to form a dough.

Step 3. Knead dough gently on a lightly floured surface. Roll out between 2 sheets of baking paper until 0.5cm thick. Using cutters, cut out shapes. Place on prepared trays. Bake for 10-15 minutes. Cool on trays. Decorate with icing and cachous (see notes).

notes

To make icing, beat egg white with a wooden spoon until frothy. Add 1¼ cups sifted pure icing sugar, 1 tablespoonful at a time, beating well after each addition. When icing is a piping consistency. Add a few drops of lemon juice and colouring. Pipe and decorate. To turn into tree decorations, make a hole in shapes before baking and thread with ribbon.

......xmas treats

x is for......

white christmas
coconut bites

makes about 36
preparation 10 minutes, plus freezing time
cooking 5 minutes

> **250g copha**
> **2 cups Rice Bubbles**
> **1 cup desiccated coconut**
> **1 cup icing sugar, sifted**
> **1 cup milk powder**
> **¾ cup sultanas**
> **½ cup chopped red and green lollies
> (red and green jelly babies)**

Step 1. Lightly grease a 20 x 30cm slice pan.
Line base and sides with baking paper. Place
copha in a small saucepan. Heat on low, stirring,
for 4-5 minutes until melted. Transfer to a jug
and allow to cool slightly.
Step 2. Meanwhile, combine all the remaining
ingredients in a large bowl. Pour in copha and
mix well.
Step 3. Press mixture firmly into pan. Freeze
15 minutes or until set, then chill until ready
to serve. Serve cut into small squares.

xmas treats

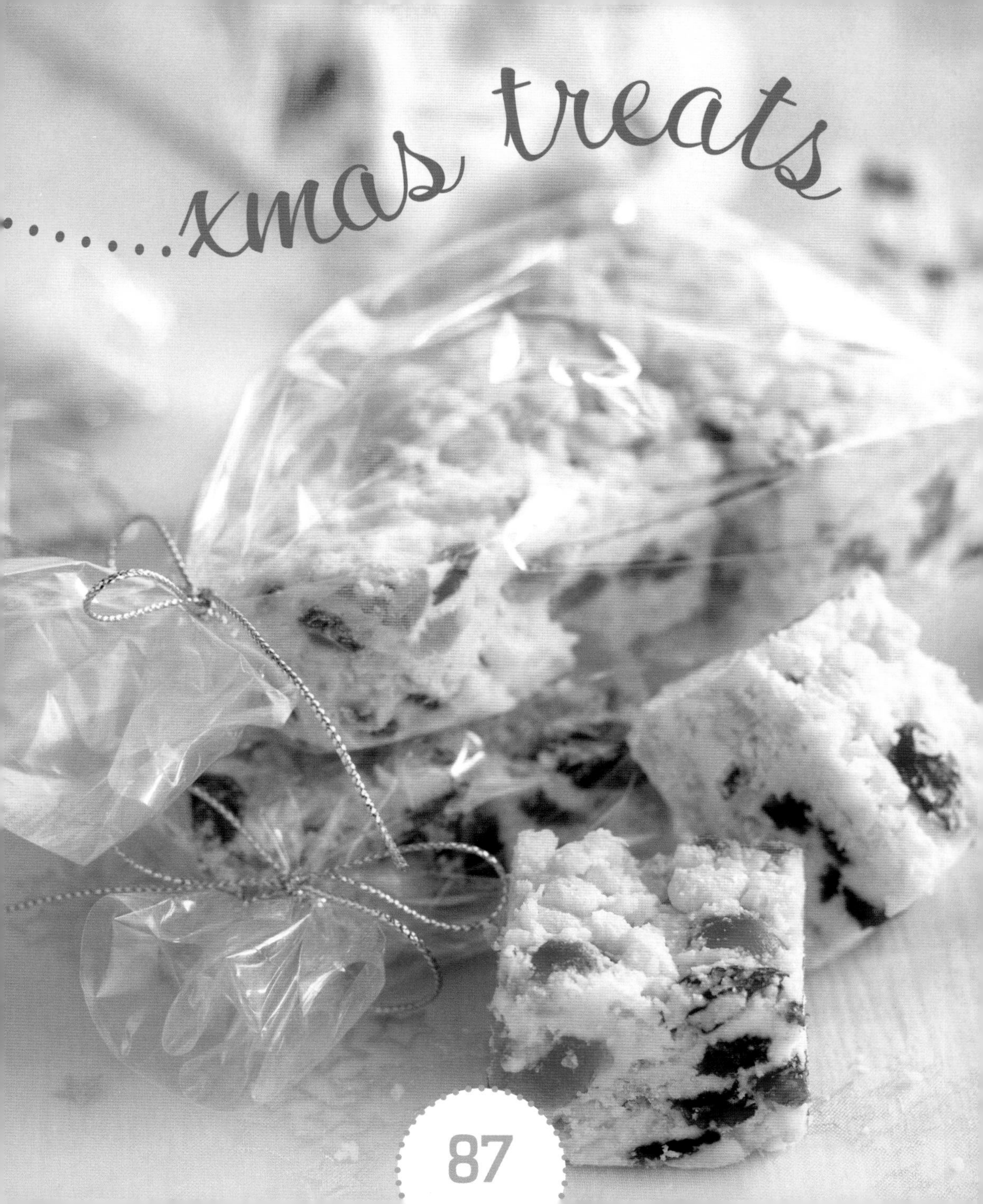

𝒳 is for......

shortbread stars

makes about 30
preparation 10 minutes
cooking 20 minutes

> **2 cups plain flour**
> **⅓ cup pure icing sugar**
> **2 tablespoons rice flour**
> **250g butter, cubed, at room temperature**
> **white chocolate buttons, to decorate**
> **icing sugar, to dust**

Step 1. Preheat oven to moderately slow, 160°C. Line 2 baking trays with baking paper. Sift flour, icing sugar and rice flour together into a bowl. Using fingertips, rub in butter until the mixture resembles breadcrumbs. Press together to form a firm dough.
Step 2. Turn onto a floured surface and knead gently. Roll out between 2 sheets baking paper until 5mm thick.
Step 3. Using a 5cm cutter, cut into stars. Arrange on prepared trays. Bake for 15-20 minutes until lightly golden. Remove from oven. Decorate some of the stars with white chocolate buttons. Cool for 5 minutes on trays. Transfer to a rack to cool completely. Dust with icing sugar to serve.

variation
To make dark-chocolate stars, add 60g melted dark chocolate in step 1. Wrap in plastic wrap and chill for 10 minutes. After baking, top with dark chocolate buttons and decorate with cachous.

89

 is for......

yoghurt berry pops

makes 8
preparation 5 minutes, plus freezing time

> **2 cups vanilla yoghurt**
> **¼ cup raspberries**
> **¼ cup blueberries**
> **½ punnet strawberries,
>   hulled, chopped**

Step 1. Measure and arrange all ingredients on work surface.
Step 2. Combine all ingredients in a large jug and pour into iceblock moulds.
Step 3. Secure lids and insert sticks. Freeze until firm. Unmould when required.

tip
To get pink yoghurt pops, purée the strawberries.

yoghurt pops

Z is for……………

...zucchini fritters...

z is for......

with guacamole

makes about 16
preparation 15 minutes
cooking 25 minutes

> 2 zucchinis, grated
> ½ cup frozen peas
> ½ cup grated tasty cheese
> ⅓ cup flour, sifted
> 2 eggs, lightly beaten
> 1 tablespoon vegetable oil
> guacamole, to serve (see note)

Step 1. In a medium bowl, combine zucchini, peas, cheese, flour and eggs. Season to taste.
Step 2. Heat oil in a large frying pan on medium. Cook tablespoonfuls of mixture in 4 batches for 2-3 minutes each side until golden.
Step 3. Drain fritters on paper towel. Top each fritter with 1 teaspoon of guacamole to serve.

note
To make guacamole, combine 1 peeled and stoned avocado and ¼ cup lite sour cream in a bowl. Season to taste.

zucchini fritters

95

.....now i know my abc.....

... won't you come ......

....and play with me?

Playdate favourites

Now you've introduced your little ones to the joy of cooking, why not involve them in the food preparation for their next playdate with friends? Little tummies need frequent refuelling, especially when they're on the run outdoors. These favourites make a great change to Vegemite sandwiches and will be a hit with mums and dads, too! Another fun idea is to make cooking an activity during the playdate, especially if it's raining outside and the kids are starting to go a little stir-crazy in the house. Here are some of Woman's Day's most-requested kids classics, plus some new tastes for you to try.

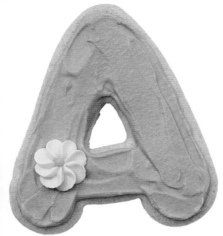

corn & cheese

lavash cases

makes 12
preparation 15 minutes
cooking 15 minutes

> **3 sheets lavash bread**
> **300g can creamed corn**
> **½ cup grated light tasty cheese**
> **¼ cup grated parmesan**
> **1 egg, beaten**
> **3 green onions, finely sliced**
> **1 tablespoon chopped parsley**

Step 1. Preheat oven to moderate, 180°C. Lightly grease a 12-hole muffin pan.
Step 2. Cut each piece of lavash into 2 even-sized squares. Press bread into prepared pan. Spray with oil.
Step 3. Combine all remaining ingredients in a bowl and season to taste. Divide evenly between bread cases.
Step 4. Bake for 10-15 minutes until golden and firm. Serve warm or cold.

tip
Try adding some chopped ham or salami to the filling.

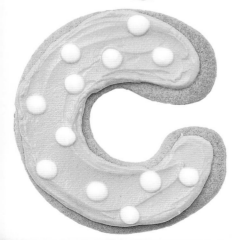

101

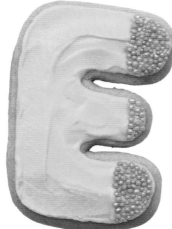

tuna & beetroot
dip with pita crisps

makes about 2 cups
preparation 5 minutes

> **450g can whole baby beetroot, drained**
> **125g packet cream cheese, at room temperature, chopped**
> **1 garlic clove, chopped**
> **185g can tuna in springwater, drained, flaked**
> **2 tablespoons chopped chives**
> **pita bread, toasted, to serve**

Step 1. Place beetroot, cream cheese and garlic in a food processor or blender. Process until smooth.
Step 2. Stir through tuna and chives. Serve the dip with pita crisps.

play... sleep... play

Tuna & Beanut Dip 15-onwards

abcd

103

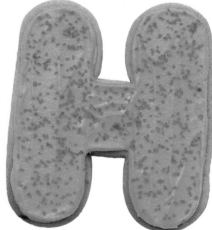

ham & cheese scrolls

makes about 10
preparation 10 minutes
cooking 15 minutes

> **2 cups self-raising flour**
> **30g butter, chopped**
> **¼ cup chopped basil**
> **½ cup milk**
> **½ cup water**

> **1 cup grated tasty cheese**
> **½ cup chopped ham**
> **½ red capsicum, seeded, chopped**
> **¼ cup chopped gherkin (optional)**

Step 1. Preheat oven to very hot, 220°C. Lightly grease a scone tray.

Step 2. Sift flour into a large bowl. Add butter. Using fingertips, rub in lightly. Stir in basil.

Step 3. Make a well in the centre of flour mixture. Pour in combined milk and water all at once, reserving 1 tablespoon. Using a palette knife, mix quickly to a soft, sticky dough. Do not over-mix.

Step 4. Turn onto a lightly floured surface. Knead lightly. Press or roll out to form a rectangle about 1cm thick.

Step 5. In a small bowl, combine cheese, ham, capsicum and gherkin, if using. Sprinkle over dough, pressing slightly.

Step 6. Roll up into a log shape. Cut into 2cm-thick slices and arrange slightly overlapping, cut side up, on prepared tray. Brush with reserved milk mixture. Bake for 12-15 minutes until scrolls sound hollow when tapped. Transfer to a wire rack. Allow scrolls to cool.

tip
For a lighter result, we used milk and water to make the base, but you can use all milk or all water. Milk is best for sweet scones or scrolls.

...play... sleep... play

105

pumpkin scones

makes 16
preparation 15 minutes
cooking 15 minutes

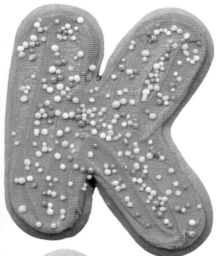

> 2½ cups self-raising flour
> ½ teaspoon mixed spice
> 30g cold butter, chopped
> 1 cup cold mashed pumpkin
> ¼ cup brown sugar
> 1 egg, beaten
> butter, honey, to serve

Step 1. Preheat oven to very hot, 220°C.
Lightly grease a scone tray.
Step 2. Sift flour and mixed spice together
into a large bowl. Add butter. Using fingertips,
rub in lightly.
Step 3. Make a well in centre of flour mixture.
Add pumpkin, sugar and egg.
Step 4. Using a palette knife, mix quickly to
a soft, sticky dough. Do not over-mix.
Step 5. Turn onto a lightly floured surface.
Knead lightly. Press or roll out to form
a round about 2cm thick. Using a 5cm cutter,
cut into 16 rounds.
Step 6. Place close together on tray. Bake for
12-15 minutes or until scones sound hollow
when tapped. Transfer to a wire rack. Allow
to cool. Serve with butter and honey.

tip
Leftover dough can be lightly kneaded and
rolled to make extra scones, but they will be
a bit harder and tougher than the first batch
due to the extra handling of dough.

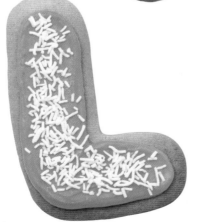

...play... sleep... play

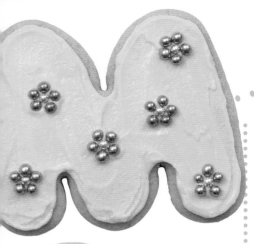

mini hot dogs

makes 6
preparation 5 minutes
cooking 10 minutes

> 6 pack par-bake dinner bread rolls
> 6 cocktail frankfurts
> ⅓ cup grated tasty cheese
> tomato sauce, to serve

Step 1. Preheat oven to hot, 200°C. Lightly grease and line a baking tray.
Step 2. Slit each roll through the top, being careful not to cut all the way through.
Step 3. Place a frankfurt in each roll. Sprinkle with cheese. Bake for 5-10 minutes until the cheese melts and frankfurts are hot. Serve with sauce and lemonade spiders (see below).

tip
You can also use chipolatas (cocktail sausages).

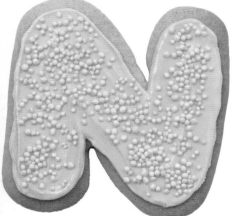

lemonade spiders

serves 6
preparation 5 minutes

> 6 large scoops vanilla ice-cream
> 1.5 litres lemonade

Step 1. Place a scoop of ice-cream into each glass. Divide lemonade between glasses and serve straightaway.

tip
You can use any type of soft drink you like.

...play... sleep... play

109

chicken bolognese
pasta pots

makes 6
preparation 20 minutes
cooking 25 minutes

> **1½ cups elbow pasta or other short pasta**
> **1 tablespoon olive oil**
> **500g chicken mince**
> **400g can diced tomatoes**
> **375g jar tomato pasta sauce**
> **100g button mushrooms, thinly sliced**
> **2 tablespoons chopped basil**
> **⅓ cup grated parmesan**
> **⅓ cup grated tasty cheese**

Step 1. Grease 6 x 1-cup ramekins.
Step 2. Cook pasta in a saucepan of boiling, salted water for 8-10 minutes until al dente. Drain well.
Step 3. Meanwhile, heat oil in a medium saucepan on high. Add chicken mince. Cook for 5-6 minutes, breaking up lumps with back of a spoon as it browns. Add diced tomatoes, tomato pasta sauce and mushroom. Simmer for 10 minutes. Stir in basil and season to taste. Stir through pasta until combined.
Step 4. Divide mixture evenly between ramekins. In a bowl, combine parmesan and tasty cheese. Sprinkle over pasta pots.
Step 5. Preheat grill to high. Place ramekins on a baking tray. Grill for 2-3 minutes until cheese melts and is golden. Serve.

...play... sleep... play

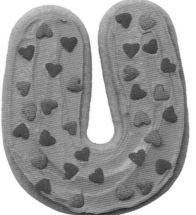

salami, tomato
& cheese melts

makes 4
preparation 5 minutes
cooking 5 minutes

> 2 English muffins, halved
> 2 tablespoons tomato paste
> 4 slices salami, chopped
> ½ small red capsicum,
  seeded, finely chopped
> ⅓ cup grated pizza
  or tasty cheese

Step 1. Preheat grill to medium. Line a baking tray with foil. Place muffin halves, cut-side up, on tray.
Step 2. Grill for 1 minute each side until lightly toasted.
Step 3. Spread tomato paste over muffin halves. Top with salami, capsicum and cheese.
Step 4. Grill for 3-4 minutes until cheese melts and is golden.

tip
Vary the ingredients – try canned pineapple rings, ham and cheese, barbecued chicken, mushroom and cheese.

...play... sleep play

113

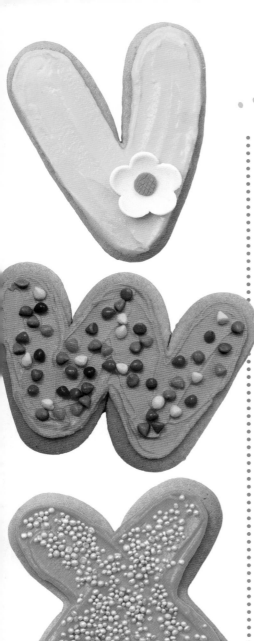

smartie biscuits

makes about 24
preparation 20 minutes
cooking 10 minutes

› **125g butter, chopped, at room temperature**
› **½ cup brown sugar**
› **½ cup caster sugar**
› **1 egg**
› **1 teaspoon vanilla extract**
› **1¼ cups plain flour**
› **¼ cup self-raising flour**
› **½ teaspoon bicarbonate of soda**
› **180g packet Smarties**

Step 1. Preheat oven to moderate, 180°C. Lightly grease 2 large baking trays.
Step 2. In a large bowl, using an electric mixer, cream butter and sugars together until light and fluffy. Beat in egg and vanilla extract until combined.
Step 3. Sift flours and bicarbonate of soda together onto a piece of paper towel. Lightly fold into butter mixture.
Step 4. Roll level tablespoonfuls of mixture into balls. Arrange on prepared trays 4cm apart. Using floured fingertips, flatten slightly. Top with Smarties.
Step 5. Bake for 10-12 minutes until golden. Allow to cool on trays for 5 minutes. Transfer to a wire rack to cool completely.

tip
These biscuits will be soft when cooked, but they will harden on cooling.

...play... sleep... play

honey jumbles

makes 20
preparation 20 minutes, plus chilling time
cooking 10 minutes

> ⅓ cup honey
> 45g butter
> 1 cup plain flour
> 1 teaspoon
  ground ginger
> ½ teaspoon
  mixed spice
> ½ teaspoon
  bicarbonate of soda

> ¼ teaspoon
  ground cloves
> 1 tablespoon milk
  ICING
> 1 egg white
> 1½ cups icing
  sugar, sifted
> few drops pink
  food colouring

Step 1. In a small saucepan, heat honey and butter together on low until melted and simmering. Allow to cool for 5 minutes.
Step 2. Sift flour, ginger, mixed spice, bicarbonate of soda and cloves together into a bowl. Make a well in the centre. Pour in honey mixture and milk. Stir until well combined. Cover with plastic wrap and chill for 30 minutes or until firm.
Step 3. Preheat oven to moderate, 180°C. Line 2 baking trays with baking paper.
Step 4. Turn dough onto a lightly floured surface. Knead, gradually working in a little extra flour, if needed, until the dough is no longer sticky.
Step 5. Divide into 2 pieces. Roll each into a sausage shape about 4cm thick. Cut into 5mm widths. Arrange on trays. Press into oval shapes.
Step 6. Bake for 8-10 minutes until they begin to crack. Allow to cool on trays.
Step 7. ICING: Place egg white in a bowl. Whisk until frothy. Gradually add icing sugar, blending until smooth. Stir in colouring. Spread evenly over biscuits. Allow to become firm.

...play... sleep... play

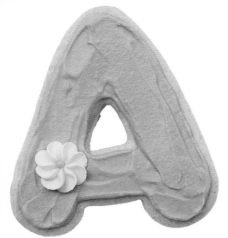

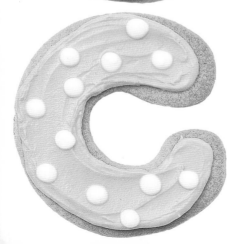

blueberry
& banana bread

makes 1 loaf
preparation 15 minutes
cooking 1 hour

> › 2 cups plain flour
> › 2 teaspoons baking powder
> › ½ teaspoon ground cinnamon
> › 1 cup brown sugar
> › 3 medium bananas, mashed
> › 125g butter, melted
> › 2 eggs, lightly beaten
> › 1 teaspoon vanilla extract
> › ¾ cup fresh or frozen blueberries

Step 1. Preheat oven to moderate, 180°C.
Lightly grease a 10 x 20cm loaf pan. Line
the base with baking paper.
Step 2. Sift flour, baking powder and cinnamon
together into a large bowl. Stir in sugar.
Step 3. In a large jug, combine banana,
butter, egg and vanilla extract. Fold into
flour mixture with blueberries until combined.
Pour mixture into prepared pan.
Step 4. Bake for 55-60 minutes or until a
skewer inserted into centre comes out clean
and dry. Cut into slices to serve.

tip
3 medium mashed bananas equals 1½ cups.

...play... sleep... play

119

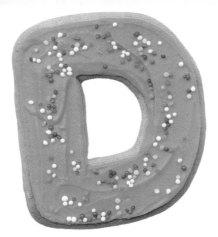

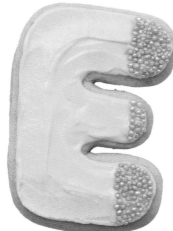

raspberry
& mango pops

makes 8
preparation 10 minutes, plus freezing time

> **1 cup frozen raspberries**
> **1 cup lemonade**
> **4 frozen mango cheeks, chopped**
> **1 cup orange juice**
> **8 paddle-pop sticks**

Step 1. Place the raspberries and lemonade in a blender and blend until smooth. Pour into 8 x 200ml iceblock moulds. Freeze for 30 minutes until partially frozen.
Step 2. Place mango and orange juice in a blender and blend until smooth. Pour over raspberry mixture. Insert a paddle-pop stick in the centre of each. Continue to freeze overnight until firm.

tip
To remove moulds, dip them into warm water for a few seconds.

...play... sleep... play

121

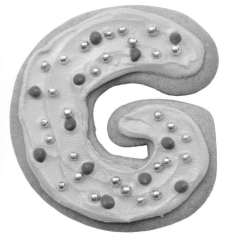

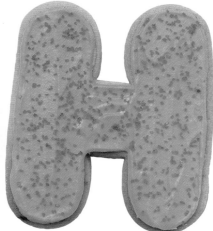

apple custard slice

makes about 16
preparation 25 minutes
cooking 1 hour

> **1 cup plain flour, sifted**
> **½ cup brown sugar**
> **½ cup desiccated coconut**
> **125g butter, melted**
> **icing sugar, to dust**
> **FILLING**
> **800g can pie apple**

> **¾ cup thickened cream**
> **2 eggs**
> **2 tablespoons caster sugar**
> **TOPPING**
> **½ cup plain flour**
> **½ cup slivered almonds**
> **⅓ cup brown sugar**
> **60g butter, melted**

Step 1. Preheat oven to moderate, 180°C. Lightly grease and line an 18 x 28cm slice pan with baking paper.

Step 2. In a bowl, combine flour, brown sugar and coconut. Blend in butter. Press mixture firmly into prepared pan. Bake for 15-20 minutes until lightly browned. Allow to cool.

Step 3. FILLING: Spread apple over base. Whisk together cream, eggs and caster sugar. Pour over apple. Bake for 20-25 minutes until firm.

Step 4. TOPPING: In a bowl, combine all the ingredients. Sprinkle evenly over slice. Bake for 12-15 minutes until golden. Allow to cool in pan. Dust with icing sugar and cut into squares to serve.

tip
If you like, you can use 1 sheet of shortcrust pastry for the base instead. Prick the base with a fork and bake for 10 minutes before covering with the filling.

...play... sleep... play

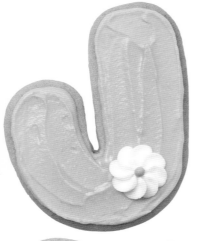

easy finger buns

makes 9
preparation 10 minutes
cooking 15 minutes

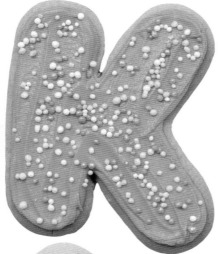

> 2 cups self-raising flour
> 30g butter, chopped
> ¼ cup sultanas
> 2 tablespoons sugar
> ¾ cup milk
> 1 egg
> 1 tablespoon just-boiled water
> 1 tablespoon caster sugar
> ICING
> 1 cup icing sugar, sifted
> 1 tablespoon just boiled water
> 1 teaspoon butter
> few drops pink food colouring

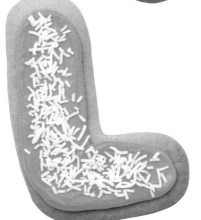

Step 1. Preheat oven to very hot, 220°C. Lightly grease a baking tray.
Step 2. Sift flour into a bowl. Add butter. Using fingertips, lightly rub in until well combined. Stir in sultanas and sugar.
Step 3. Make a well in the centre of flour mixture. In a jug, whisk together milk and egg. Pour into well all at once, reserving 1 tablespoon. Using a palette knife, quickly mix to a soft, sticky dough. Do not over-mix.
Step 4. Turn onto a lightly floured surface. Knead lightly. Break dough into 9 even-sized pieces. Roll into finger-bun shapes.
Step 5. Place buns close together on prepared tray. Brush with reserved milk mixture. Bake for 12-15 minutes until buns sound hollow when tapped. Remove from oven.
Step 6. In a jug, combine water and caster sugar. Brush over buns. Transfer to a wire rack. Allow to cool.
Step 7. ICING: In a bowl, combine icing sugar, water and butter. Add food colouring. Mix well. Spread on buns. Serve with or without butter.

...play... sleep... play

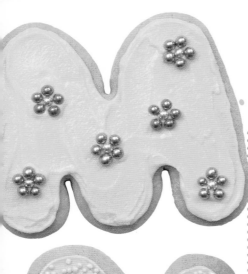

muesli bubble bars

makes 16
preparation 10 minutes, plus chilling time
cooking 5 minutes

> **50g butter**
> **250g packet marshmallows**
> **2 cups Rice Bubbles**
> **¾ cup rolled oats**
> **½ cup shredded coconut**
> **½ cup dried cranberries**
> **⅓ cup pepitas**

Step 1. Lightly grease an 18 x 28cm slice pan.
Line base and sides with baking paper.
Step 2. In a medium saucepan, combine
butter and marshmallows. Heat on low for
5-6 minutes, stirring, until melted and smooth.
Step 3. In a large bowl, combine remaining
ingredients. Add marshmallow mixture.
Working quickly, mix well and press into
prepared pan. Using a wet spatula, flatten top.
Step 4. Chill for 2-3 hours until firm. While still
in pan, cut into bars. You can store in an airtight
container in the fridge for up to 1 week.

tip
Pepitas are edible pumpkin seeds that have
had their white hull removed. They are green
with a delicate nutty flavour.

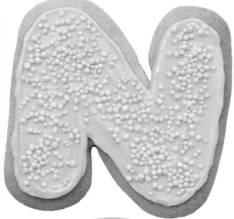

...play... sleep... play

fruit kebabs
with passionfruit dip

makes 12
preparation 20 minutes

> **1 punnet strawberries**
> **½ rockmelon, peeled, seeded, cut into chunks**
> **¼ seedless watermelon, cut into chunks**
> **¼ pineapple, cut into chunks**
> **2 bananas, thickly sliced**
> **2 kiwifruit, peeled, quartered**
> **12 bamboo skewers or straws**
> **PASSIONFRUIT DIPPING SAUCE**
> **1 cup vanilla yoghurt**
> **¼ cup passionfruit pulp**

Step 1. Thread fruit chunks alternately onto skewers. Set aside.
Step 2. PASSIONFRUIT DIPPING SAUCE: In a jug, combine yoghurt and passionfruit. Drizzle over fruit kebabs to serve.

tip
For a delicious variation, replace the passionfruit in the dipping sauce with 1 tablespoon of honey.

play... sleep... play

129

watermelon sorbet

makes 6 cups
preparation 5 minutes, plus overnight freezing
cooking 15 minutes

> 1 cup caster sugar
> 1½ cups water
> 2kg seedless watermelon,
  skin removed, chopped
> 4 egg whites
> 6 paper cups
> 6 paddle-pop sticks

Step 1. Combine the sugar and water in
a medium saucepan. Stir over a low heat
until the sugar dissolves. Simmer, without
stirring, for 10 minutes until the mixture
thickens. Remove from the heat and allow
to cool in pan.
Step 2. Purée watermelon in a blender or
food processor. Pour through a sieve. Add
to the syrup and stir to combine.
Step 3. Pour mixture into a metal cake pan,
cover with foil and freeze until almost set.
Transfer to a chilled bowl. Add egg whites and
beat with an electric mixer for 2-3 minutes until
all the ice particles have broken up.
Step 4. Divide the sorbet evenly between
the paper cups. Insert a paddle-pop stick
in the centre of each and continue to freeze
overnight until firm.

131

choc-chip
pikelets

makes about 20
preparation 5 minutes
cooking 10 minutes

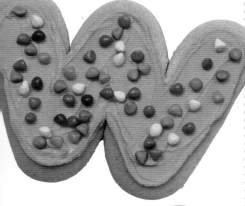

> 1 cup self-raising flour
> ½ cup finely chopped milk chocolate
>   or choc chips
> 2 tablespoons caster sugar
> 1 cup milk
> 1 egg
> 65g butter, melted
> whipped cream, to serve

Step 1. Sift flour into a bowl. Stir in chocolate and sugar.
Step 2. In a jug, whisk together milk, egg and 50g butter until combined. Gradually add to flour mixture, whisking until smooth.
Step 3. Heat a large non-stick frying pan on medium. Brush with a little of the remaining melted butter.
Step 4. Drop level tablespoonfuls of batter into pan and cook for 1-2 minutes, until bubbles appear on the surface. Turn and cook the other side for 1 minute or until golden.
Step 5. Repeat with remaining batter, brushing the pan with butter between batches. Serve pikelets with cream.

tip
As the pikletes are made with self-raising flour, there's no need to rest the batter before you cook them.

...play... sleep... play

133

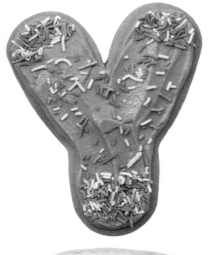

sushi ham balls

makes 18
preparation 25 minutes
cooking 25 minutes

> **1 cup sushi rice, rinsed, drained**
> **1¼ cups water**
> **2 tablespoons sushi vinegar**
> **½ small avocado, finely diced**
> **⅓ Lebanese cucumber, finely diced**
> **100g shaved smoked ham, cut into 3cm strips**
> **lettuce leaves, to serve**

Step 1. Place rice in a saucepan and cover with water. Bring to the boil on high. Reduce heat to low. Cover and simmer for 15 minutes. Remove from heat and set aside, covered, for 10 minutes.
Step 2. Line a baking tray with baking paper. Transfer rice to a bowl. Stir through sushi vinegar. Spread rice on a tray to cool.
Step 3. Using wet hands, shape tablespoonfuls of rice into balls. Poke your finger into centre of each ball and insert a piece of avocado and cucumber. Reshape the rice around filling.
Step 4. Wrap a strip of ham around each rice ball. Serve with lettuce leaves.

tip
These are great to take to school. Place lettuce leaves in a lunch box with a secure lid and top with sushi balls.

...play... sleep... play

135

playing it safe......

Here are some basic tips for playing it safe in the kitchen with kids. These simple guidelines will ensure the experience stays fun for everyone.

before you begin

> **Make sure there is an adult supervising in the kitchen at all times. Also make sure you read the recipe through together a few times before you start preparing. Have all the ingredients and utensils you need ready to go.**

clean hands

> Hands should always be washed with soap and warm water (don't forget your fingernails) and dried on a clean towel or paper towel. This is extremely important when you are handling uncooked food. Before making sandwiches, cutting a fruit salad or tossing salad vegetables, always wash your hands thoroughly. If someone has a cut on their hand, they should wear disposable gloves. Hands should always be washed after touching any uncooked meat, seafood or poultry.

personal hygiene

> No-one should touch their hair or mouth, or leave the kitchen to do something else, without washing their hands again before touching any food. Remember to stay out of the kitchen if you're sick.

clothing to wear

> Kids (and adults!) should wear short-sleeved or tight-fitting, long-sleeved tops. Loose-fitting ones can drop into the food, or worse, catch fire over a hot stove.

feet first

> Everyone should wear closed-toed shoes when cooking (more than one chef has dropped a sharp knife, point-first, onto his or her toes). It's not a bad idea to wear non-slip shoes as well.

136

defrosting
your meat

> Always thaw meat, seafood and poultry, covered, in the refrigerator. In a pinch, you can defrost these items in your microwave oven, but take care because some outside edges of the meat can actually cook. Place meat on a tray in the refrigerator as it defrosts to stop it dripping onto other food.

keep hair
out of the way

> You should tie long hair back to keep it from falling into the food or onto food preparation surfaces. It will also prevent singeing from any wayward strands. This is why most chefs wear hats!

taste the food

> It's a good idea to taste food as you prepare it, to test for flavour, but don't taste from the stirring spoon or salad fork, then return it to the saucepan or serving bowl. Use different, clean cutlery every time you taste. And, don't add salt to enhance the flavour – your idea of perfect seasoning may be far too much for someone else.

tidy up
as you go

> Keep work surfaces clean and tidy as you go. Wipe up any spills or grease spots that occur during cooking. Never use the same cloth to wipe your hands and to clean the benchtops. Rinse the cloth constantly in hot soapy water. And, if you wash any equipment you've used, you can use it again to make something else. Even if you don't use it again, at least the food won't cement itself to the bottom of the utensils.

put stuff away

> Put the food you've finished with back in the refrigerator or pantry, checking first to make sure that lids are on tight. If you're putting away any uncooked meat, seafood or poultry, ensure it's wrapped tightly in plastic wrap or placed in a sealable bag or an airtight container. The same applies to raw vegetables. Wrap them tightly and return them to the crisper in the fridge.

index

139

index

conversion charts....

measures

> One Australian metric measuring cup holds 250ml, one Australian metric tablespoon holds 20ml, one Australian metric teaspoon holds 5ml.
> The difference between one country's measuring cups and another's is within a two- or three-teaspoon variance (only 10 or 15ml), and will not affect your cooking results. Most countries, including the US, the UK and New Zealand use a 15ml tablespoon.
> All cup and spoon measurements are level. The most accurate way of measuring dry ingredients is to weigh them. When measuring liquids, use a clear glass or plastic jug with the metric markings at eye level.
> In this book, we used large eggs with an average weight of 60g each.

liquid measures

METRIC	IMPERIAL
30ml	1 fluid oz
60ml	2 fluid oz
100ml	3 fluid oz
125ml	4 fluid oz
150ml	5 fluid oz (¼ pint/1 gill)
190ml	6 fluid oz
250ml	8 fluid oz
300ml	10 fluid oz (½ pint)
500ml	16 fluid oz
600ml	20 fluid oz (1 pint)
1000ml (1 litre)	1¾ pints

oven temperatures

> These oven temperatures are only a guide for conventional ovens. For fan-forced ovens, check the manufacturer's manual.

	° C (CELSIUS)	° F (FAHRENHEIT)	GAS MARK
Very slow	120	250	½
Slow	150	275-300	1-2
Moderately slow	160	325	3
Moderate	180	350-375	4-5
Moderately hot	190	400	6
Hot	200	425-450	7-8
Very hot	220	475	9

dry measures

METRIC	IMPERIAL
15g	½oz
30g	1oz
60g	2oz
90g	3oz
125g	4oz (¼lb)
155g	5oz
185g	6oz
220g	7oz
250g	8oz (½lb)
280g	9oz
315g	10oz
345g	11oz
375g	12oz (¾lb)
410g	13oz
440g	14oz
470g	15oz
500g	16oz (1lb)
750g	24oz (1½lb)
1kg	32oz (2lb)

length measures

METRIC	IMPERIAL
3mm	⅛in
6mm	¼in
1cm	½in
2cm	¾in
2.5cm	1in
5cm	2in
6cm	2½in
8cm	3in
10cm	4in
13cm	5in
15cm	6in
18cm	7in
20cm	8in
23cm	9in
25cm	10in
28cm	11in
30cm	12in (1ft)

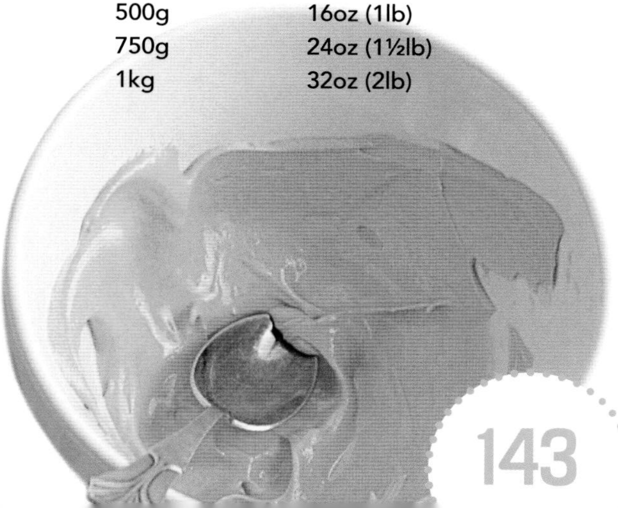

Editor Alana House
Art Director Tessa Thomas
Food Director Jennene Plummer
Food Editor Sharon Reeve
Chief Sub-editor Amanda Shaw
Digital Prepress Specialist John Ruperto

ACP BOOKS
General Manager Christine Whiston
Director of sales Brian Cearnes
Marketing manager Bridget Cody

ACP Books are published by ACP Magazines, a division of PBL Media Pty Limited
Group publisher, Women's lifestyle Pat Ingram
Director of sales, Women's lifestyle Lynette Phillips
Commercial manager, Women's lifestyle Seymour Cohen
Marketing director, Women's lifestyle Matthew Dominello
Public relations manager, Women's lifestyle Hannah Deveraux
Creative director, Events, Women's Lifestyle Luke Bonnaro
Research director, Women's lifestyle Justin Stone
ACP Magazines, Chief executive officer Scott Lorson
Editor Woman's Day Amy Sinclair
Editorial Director (weekly titles) Louisa Hatfield
PBL Media Chief Executive Officer Ian Law

Cover photographer: Brett Stevens Cover stylist: Michelle Noerianto
Other photography: Ian Hoffstetter, Rob Lowe, Andre Martin, Cath Muscat, Rob Shaw, Brett Stevens, John Paul Urizar
Other styling: Kate Brown, Jane Collins, Kate Nixon, Michelle Noerianto, Jennene Plummer, Sharon Reeve
Food preparation: Dixie Elliott, Nicole Jennings, Tracy Rutherford, Mandy Sinclair

Props used: Aprons: Shack (on cover); bowls & mini rolling pins: Wheel & Barrow (pages 8-9); plate: Bison Homewares (page 19).
The publishers would like to thank all other suppliers of props used in this book, which have been previously credited.

Printed by Toppan Printing Co (Aust) Pty Ltd, Level 10, 179 Elizabeth Street, Sydney NSW 2000, Australia
Produced by ACP Books, a division of ACP Magazines Ltd, 54 Park Street, Sydney; GPO Box 4088, Sydney, NSW 1028
Ph: (02) 9282 8618 Fax: (02) 9267 9438
www.acpbooks.com.au acpbooks@acpmagazines.com.au
To order books, phone 136 116 (within Australia) Send recipe enquiries to recipeenquiries@acpmagazines.com.au

AUSTRALIA: Distributed by Network Services, GPO Box 4088, Sydney, NSW 1028 Ph: (02) 9282 8777 Fax: (02) 9264 3278
UNITED KINGDOM: Distributed by Australian Consolidated Press (UK), Moulton Park Business Centre, Red House Rd, Moulton Park,
Northampton, NN3 6AQ Ph: (01604) 497 531 Fax: (01604) 497 533 books@acpmedia.co.uk
CANADA: Distributed by Whitecap Books Ltd, 351 Lynn Ave, North Vancouver, BC, V7J 2C4
Ph: (604) 980 9852 Fax: (604) 980 8197 customerservice@whitecap.ca www.whitecap.ca
NEW ZEALAND: Distributed by Netlink Distribution Company, phone (9) 366 9966 ask@ndc.co.nz
SOUTH AFRICA: Distributed by PSD Promotions (Pty) Ltd, Ph: (27 11) 392 6065/6/7 Fax: (27 11) 392 6079/80 orders@psdprom.co.za

The ABC of Kids Cooking: Woman's Day
Includes index
ISBN 978 1 86396 839 3 (pbk)
1. Cookery - juvenile literature. 2. Kids' cooking.
I. House, Alana. II Title: Woman's Day
641.5123
© ACP Publishing Pty Limited 2008
ABN 18 053 273 546